W9-BGU-233

Date: 4/13/20

J BIO TAFT
Rumsch, BreAnn,
William Taft /

DISCARDED:

OUTDATED, REDUNDANT
MATERIAL

PALM BEACH COUNTY
LIBRARY SYSTEM
3650 SUMMIT BLVD.
WEST PALM BEACH, FL 33406

The ★ UNITED STATES ★ PRESIDENTS

William

TAFT

BreAnn Rumsch

Big Buddy Books
An Imprint of Abdo Publishing
abdopublishing.com

abdopublishing.com

Published by Abdo Publishing, a division of ABDO, PO Box 398166, Minneapolis, Minnesota 55439. Copyright © 2017 by Abdo Consulting Group, Inc. International copyrights reserved in all countries. No part of this book may be reproduced in any form without written permission from the publisher. Big Buddy Books™ is a trademark and logo of Abdo Publishing.

Printed in the United States of America, North Mankato, Minnesota
062016
092016

THIS BOOK CONTAINS
RECYCLED MATERIALS

Design: Sarah DeYoung, Mighty Media, Inc.
Production: Mighty Media, Inc.
Editor: Liz Salzmann
Cover Photograph: Getty Images
Interior Photographs: AP Images (pp. 7, 27); Corbis (pp. 6, 13, 15, 19, 21); Getty Images (pp. 5, 6, 11); iStockphoto (p. 29); Library of Congress (pp. 9, 17, 23); North Wind (pp. 7, 25)

Cataloging-in-Publication Data

Names: Rumsch, BreAnn, author.
Title: William Taft / by BreAnn Rumsch.
Description: Minneapolis, MN : Abdo Publishing, [2017] | Series: United States
    presidents | Includes bibliographical references and index.
Identifiers: LCCN 2015957559 | ISBN 9781680781175 (lib. bdg.) |
    ISBN 9781680775372 (ebook)
Subjects: LCSH: Taft, William H. (William Howard), 1857-1930--Juvenile
    literature. | Presidents--United States--Biography--Juvenile literature. |
    United States--Politics and government--1909-1913--Juvenile literature.
Classification: DDC 973.912/092 [B]--dc23
LC record available at http://lccn.loc.gov/2015957559

Contents

William Taft

William Taft was the twenty-seventh president of the United States. During Taft's presidency, the **Republican** Party was **divided**. Taft tried to work with both sides of the party. But they could not get along.

After leaving the White House, Taft became a teacher. Then, he was made **chief justice** of the US **Supreme Court**. Taft is the only person in US history to have been both president and chief justice. Taft served his country well.

Timeline

1857
William Howard Taft was born on September 15 in Cincinnati, Ohio.

1886
On June 19, Taft married Helen "Nellie" Herron.

1881
Taft became a **prosecuting attorney** in Hamilton County, Ohio.

1901
Taft became governor of the Philippines.

1912

Taft lost the presidential election to Woodrow Wilson.

1921

President Warren G. Harding asked Taft to be **chief justice** of the US **Supreme Court**.

1909

On March 4, Taft became the twenty-seventh US president.

1930

In February, Taft left the Supreme Court. William Taft died on March 8.

7

Young Will

William Howard Taft was born in Cincinnati, Ohio, on September 15, 1857. Everyone called him Will. Will's parents were Louise and Alphonso Taft.

Will studied hard in school. After high school, he attended Yale University in Connecticut. He finished in 1878.

★ FAST FACTS ★

Born: September 15, 1857

Wife: Helen Herron (1861–1943)

Children: three

Political Party: Republican

Age at Inauguration: 51

Years Served: 1909–1913

Vice President: James S. Sherman

Died: March 8, 1930, age 72

Alphonso Taft was
a successful judge.

Work and Family

After Yale, Taft attended the Cincinnati Law School in Ohio. In 1881, Taft became a **prosecuting attorney** in Hamilton County, Ohio.

Several years before, Taft had met Helen Herron. The couple married on June 19, 1886. The next year, Taft became a judge on the Ohio **Superior Court**.

In 1890, President Benjamin Harrison made Taft the US **solicitor general**. Two years later, President Harrison made him a judge on the US **Circuit Court**.

Helen Herron Taft
was called Nellie.

Governor Taft

In 1898, the Philippine Islands became a US territory. In 1901, Taft became the first nonmilitary governor of the Philippines. Governor Taft did much for the Filipino people. He built roads, harbors, and schools.

Taft also created a court system in the Philippines. Taft hoped that one day the Filipinos would run their own government. The Tafts enjoyed the Philippines. And they were well-liked by the Filipinos.

Governor Taft (*center*) worked with a commission to establish a new government and laws in the Philippines.

Secretary Taft

In 1903, President Theodore Roosevelt asked Taft to be his **secretary of war**. That year, the United States and Panama made an agreement. It said the United States could construct the **Panama Canal**. The United States would also control the area around the construction site.

In 1904, Taft returned to Washington, DC, to begin work as secretary of war. During this time, he oversaw the construction of the Panama Canal. Taft also worked to establish a government in the area.

Taft often traveled to Panama to inspect the construction of the Panama Canal.

As **secretary of war**, Taft visited Japan to help Roosevelt work on the **Treaty** of Portsmouth. This treaty ended a war between Russia and Japan in 1905. He also went to Cuba in 1906. There, he helped stop a war.

In 1908, Roosevelt announced that he would not seek reelection. The **Republican** Party chose Taft to run for president. He ran against **Democrat** William Jennings Bryan. Taft easily won the election.

> ★ **DID YOU KNOW?** ★
>
> On April 14, 1910, Taft became the first president to throw out the first ball to open the Major League Baseball season.

A campaign poster for Taft promised voters "Good Times."

President Taft

Taft took office on March 4, 1909. Sadly, he had trouble from the start. One thing Taft wanted to do was lower **tariffs**.

The House of **Representatives** passed a bill to lower tariffs. But the Senate made changes to the bill. Their changes kept many of the tariffs high.

Although he didn't like the changes, Taft signed the act anyway. This angered many **Republicans**. They felt Taft had gone back on his word to lower tariffs.

After he took office, Taft and his wife rode in a horse-drawn carriage from the Capitol to the White House.

Soon, more trouble followed. Gifford Pinchot was chief of the US Forest Service. He said **Secretary of the Interior** Richard A. Ballinger was dishonest. Taft didn't believe Pinchot.

A special group of congressmen cleared Ballinger's name. The following year, Taft fired Pinchot. However, some **Republicans** believed Pinchot's claims. They grew unhappy with Taft. They began to turn to Theodore Roosevelt as their true leader.

SUPREME COURT APPOINTMENTS

Horace H. Lurton: 1910

Charles Evans Hughes: 1910

Willis Van Devanter: 1911

Joseph R. Lamar: 1911

Edward Douglass White: 1910

Mahlon Pitney: 1912

Gifford Pinchot

Although he had trouble with the **Republican** Party, Taft had some success with Congress. He helped form the **Tariff** Board and broke up many **trusts**. Taft took the first steps toward establishing a **budget** for the country.

In 1912, Taft established the US Children's **Bureau**. This bureau helped children have better lives. That same year, Taft made Arizona and New Mexico US states. And, Alaska became a US territory.

★ DID YOU KNOW? ★

Taft was the first president to own a car.

President Taft worked hard to make changes for the better. But party disagreements took attention away from his efforts.

Tough Campaign

In 1912, the **Republican** Party was still **divided**. One group of Republicans chose President Taft to run for a second term. The other group formed a separate party. That party chose Roosevelt to run for president.

The **Democratic** Party chose Governor Woodrow Wilson of New Jersey. With the Republican Party divided, it had little power. So Wilson easily won the election.

PRESIDENT TAFT'S CABINET

March 4, 1909–March 4, 1913

★ **STATE:** Philander C. Knox
★ **TREASURY:** Franklin MacVeagh
★ **WAR:** Jacob M. Dickinson,
  Henry L. Stimson (from May 22, 1911)
★ **NAVY:** George von L. Meyer
★ **ATTORNEY GENERAL:**
  George W. Wickersham
★ **INTERIOR:** Richard A. Ballinger,
  Walter L. Fisher (from March 7, 1911)
★ **AGRICULTURE:** James Wilson
★ **COMMERCE AND LABOR:**
  Charles Nagel

President Taft signed
an act to approve
Arizona's statehood.

Chief Justice

After leaving the White House, Taft taught law school. But he continued to follow **politics** in Washington, DC. In 1921, President Warren G. Harding asked Taft to be **chief justice** of the US **Supreme Court**.

When Taft joined the Supreme Court, it was overloaded with cases. So, he asked Congress to give the Supreme Court more freedom in choosing its cases. They could get rid of backed-up cases and run more smoothly. To this end, Congress passed the Judges Act in 1925.

Chief Justice Taft served on the Supreme Court from 1921 to 1930.

In February 1930, Taft left the **Supreme Court**. On March 8, William Taft died from heart problems. He was buried in Arlington National **Cemetery** in Virginia.

As president, Taft was successful in many ways. Yet, Taft's term was marked by fighting within the **Republican** Party. This weakened Taft's power as president. Yet as **chief justice**, William Taft was an important American leader.

★ DID YOU KNOW? ★

William Taft was the first president to be buried in Arlington National Cemetery. Only one other president, John F. Kennedy, has been buried there since.

Taft oversaw the planning
and initial construction
of the US Supreme Court
building in Washington, DC.

Office of the President

Branches of Government

The US government has three branches. They are the executive, legislative, and judicial branches. Each branch has some power over the others. This is called a system of checks and balances.

★ Executive Branch

The executive branch enforces laws. It is made up of the president, the vice president, and the president's cabinet. The president represents the United States around the world. He or she also signs bills into law and leads the military.

★ Legislative Branch

The legislative branch makes laws, maintains the military, and regulates trade. It also has the power to declare war. This branch includes the Senate and the House of Representatives. Together, these two houses form Congress.

★ Judicial Branch

The judicial branch interprets laws. It is made up of district courts, courts of appeals, and the Supreme Court. District courts try cases. Sometimes people disagree with a trial's outcome. Then he or she may appeal. If a court of appeals supports the ruling, a person may appeal to the Supreme Court.

Qualifications for Office

To be president, a candidate must be at least 35 years old. The person must be a natural-born US citizen. He or she must also have lived in the United States for at least 14 years.

Electoral College

The US presidential election is an indirect election. Voters from each state choose electors. These electors represent their state in the Electoral College. Each elector has one electoral vote. Electors cast their vote for the candidate with the highest number of votes from people in their state. A candidate must receive the majority of Electoral College votes to win.

Term of Office

Each president may be elected to two four-year terms. The presidential election is held on the Tuesday after the first Monday in November. The president is sworn in on January 20 of the following year. At that time, he or she takes the oath of office.
It states:

> I do solemnly swear (or affirm) that I will faithfully execute the office of President of the United States, and will to the best of my ability, preserve, protect and defend the Constitution of the United States.

31

Line of Succession

The Presidential Succession Act of 1947 states who becomes president if the president cannot serve. The vice president is first in the line. Next are the Speaker of the House and the President Pro Tempore of the Senate. It may happen that none of these individuals is able to serve. Then the office falls to the president's cabinet members. They would take office in the order in which each department was created:

Secretary of State

Secretary of the Treasury

Secretary of Defense

Attorney General

Secretary of the Interior

Secretary of Agriculture

Secretary of Commerce

Secretary of Labor

Secretary of Health and Human Services

Secretary of Housing and Urban Development

Secretary of Transportation

Secretary of Energy

Secretary of Education

Secretary of Veterans Affairs

Secretary of Homeland Security

Benefits

★ While in office, the president receives a salary. It is $400,000 per year. He or she lives in the White House. The president also has 24-hour Secret Service protection.

★ The president may travel on a Boeing 747 jet. This special jet is called Air Force One. It can hold 70 passengers. It has kitchens, a dining room, sleeping areas, and more. Air Force One can fly halfway around the world before needing to refuel. It can even refuel in flight!

★ When the president travels by car, he or she uses Cadillac One. It is a Cadillac Deville that has been modified. The car has heavy armor and communications systems. The president may even take Cadillac One along when visiting other countries.

★ The president also travels on a helicopter. It is called Marine One. It may also be taken along when the president visits other countries.

★ Sometimes the president needs to get away with family and friends. Camp David is the official presidential retreat. It is located in Maryland. The US Navy maintains the retreat. The US Marine Corps keeps it secure. The camp offers swimming, tennis, golf, and hiking.

★ When the president leaves office, he or she receives lifetime Secret Service protection. He or she also receives a yearly pension of $203,700. The former president also receives money for office space, supplies, and staff.

PRESIDENTS AND THEIR TERMS

PRESIDENT	PARTY	TOOK OFFICE	LEFT OFFICE	TERMS SERVED	VICE PRESIDENT
George Washington	None	April 30, 1789	March 4, 1797	Two	John Adams
John Adams	Federalist	March 4, 1797	March 4, 1801	One	Thomas Jefferson
Thomas Jefferson	Democratic-Republican	March 4, 1801	March 4, 1809	Two	Aaron Burr, George Clinton
James Madison	Democratic-Republican	March 4, 1809	March 4, 1817	Two	George Clinton, Elbridge Gerry
James Monroe	Democratic-Republican	March 4, 1817	March 4, 1825	Two	Daniel D. Tompkins
John Quincy Adams	Democratic-Republican	March 4, 1825	March 4, 1829	One	John C. Calhoun
Andrew Jackson	Democrat	March 4, 1829	March 4, 1837	Two	John C. Calhoun, Martin Van Buren
Martin Van Buren	Democrat	March 4, 1837	March 4, 1841	One	Richard M. Johnson
William H. Harrison	Whig	March 4, 1841	April 4, 1841	Died During First Term	John Tyler
John Tyler	Whig	April 6, 1841	March 4, 1845	Completed Harrison's Term	Office Vacant
James K. Polk	Democrat	March 4, 1845	March 4, 1849	One	George M. Dallas
Zachary Taylor	Whig	March 5, 1849	July 9, 1850	Died During First Term	Millard Fillmore

PRESIDENT	PARTY	TOOK OFFICE	LEFT OFFICE	TERMS SERVED	VICE PRESIDENT
Millard Fillmore	Whig	July 10, 1850	March 4, 1853	Completed Taylor's Term	Office Vacant
Franklin Pierce	Democrat	March 4, 1853	March 4, 1857	One	William R.D. King
James Buchanan	Democrat	March 4, 1857	March 4, 1861	One	John C. Breckinridge
Abraham Lincoln	Republican	March 4, 1861	April 15, 1865	Served One Term, Died During Second Term	Hannibal Hamlin, Andrew Johnson
Andrew Johnson	Democrat	April 15, 1865	March 4, 1869	Completed Lincoln's Second Term	Office Vacant
Ulysses S. Grant	Republican	March 4, 1869	March 4, 1877	Two	Schuyler Colfax, Henry Wilson
Rutherford B. Hayes	Republican	March 3, 1877	March 4, 1881	One	William A. Wheeler
James A. Garfield	Republican	March 4, 1881	September 19, 1881	Died During First Term	Chester Arthur
Chester Arthur	Republican	September 20, 1881	March 4, 1885	Completed Garfield's Term	Office Vacant
Grover Cleveland	Democrat	March 4, 1885	March 4, 1889	One	Thomas A. Hendricks
Benjamin Harrison	Republican	March 4, 1889	March 4, 1893	One	Levi P. Morton
Grover Cleveland	Democrat	March 4, 1893	March 4, 1897	One	Adlai E. Stevenson
William McKinley	Republican	March 4, 1897	September 14, 1901	Served One Term, Died During Second Term	Garret A. Hobart, Theodore Roosevelt

PRESIDENT	PARTY	TOOK OFFICE	LEFT OFFICE	TERMS SERVED	VICE PRESIDENT
Theodore Roosevelt	Republican	September 14, 1901	March 4, 1909	Completed McKinley's Second Term, Served One Term	Office Vacant, Charles Fairbanks
William Taft	Republican	March 4, 1909	March 4, 1913	One	James S. Sherman
Woodrow Wilson	Democrat	March 4, 1913	March 4, 1921	Two	Thomas R. Marshall
Warren G. Harding	Republican	March 4, 1921	August 2, 1923	Died During First Term	Calvin Coolidge
Calvin Coolidge	Republican	August 3, 1923	March 4, 1929	Completed Harding's Term, Served One Term	Office Vacant, Charles Dawes
Herbert Hoover	Republican	March 4, 1929	March 4, 1933	One	Charles Curtis
Franklin D. Roosevelt	Democrat	March 4, 1933	April 12, 1945	Served Three Terms, Died During Fourth Term	John Nance Garner, Henry A. Wallace, Harry S. Truman
Harry S. Truman	Democrat	April 12, 1945	January 20, 1953	Completed Roosevelt's Fourth Term, Served One Term	Office Vacant, Alben Barkley
Dwight D. Eisenhower	Republican	January 20, 1953	January 20, 1961	Two	Richard Nixon
John F. Kennedy	Democrat	January 20, 1961	November 22, 1963	Died During First Term	Lyndon B. Johnson
Lyndon B. Johnson	Democrat	November 22, 1963	January 20, 1969	Completed Kennedy's Term, Served One Term	Office Vacant, Hubert H. Humphrey
Richard Nixon	Republican	January 20, 1969	August 9, 1974	Completed First Term, Resigned During Second Term	Spiro T. Agnew, Gerald Ford

PRESIDENT	PARTY	TOOK OFFICE	LEFT OFFICE	TERMS SERVED	VICE PRESIDENT
Gerald Ford	Republican	August 9, 1974	January 20, 1977	Completed Nixon's Second Term	Nelson A. Rockefeller
Jimmy Carter	Democrat	January 20, 1977	January 20, 1981	One	Walter Mondale
Ronald Reagan	Republican	January 20, 1981	January 20, 1989	Two	George H.W. Bush
George H.W. Bush	Republican	January 20, 1989	January 20, 1993	One	Dan Quayle
Bill Clinton	Democrat	January 20, 1993	January 20, 2001	Two	Al Gore
George W. Bush	Republican	January 20, 2001	January 20, 2009	Two	Dick Cheney
Barack Obama	Democrat	January 20, 2009	January 20, 2017	Two	Joe Biden

"Too many people do not care what happens as long as it does not happen to them." William Taft

★ WRITE TO THE PRESIDENT ★

You may write to the president at:
The White House
1600 Pennsylvania Avenue NW
Washington, DC 20500

You may e-mail the president at:
comments@whitehouse.gov

37

Glossary

budget—a plan for how much money will be earned and spent during a particular period of time.

bureau (BYUR-oh)—an office or department that provides services for the public.

cemetery—a place where the dead are buried.

chief justice—the head judge of the US Supreme Court.

circuit court—a court whose judges travel around an area to hear cases.

Democrat—a member of the Democratic political party.

divide—to separate into two parts.

Panama Canal—a human-made, narrow canal across Panama that connects the Atlantic and Pacific oceans.

politics—the art or science of government. Something referring to politics is political. A person who is active in politics is a politician.

prosecuting attorney—a lawyer who represents the government in court cases.

representative—someone chosen in an election to act or speak for the people who voted for him or her.

Republican—a member of the Republican political party.

secretary of the interior—a member of the president's cabinet who manages public lands and protects wildlife.

secretary of war—a member of the president's cabinet who handled the military and national defense.

solicitor general—the chief law officer of the United States.

superior court—a court that hears important cases from throughout a state.

Supreme Court—the highest, most powerful court of a nation or a state.

tariff—the taxes a government puts on imported or exported goods.

treaty—an agreement made between two or more groups.

trust—a group of companies that form an agreement to use business practices that are sometimes unfair.

★ WEBSITES ★

To learn more about the US Presidents, visit **booklinks.abdopublishing.com**. These links are routinely monitored and updated to provide the most current information available.

Index